The Day of the Disaster

HURRICANE HUGO

Written By: Sue L. Hamilton

NOTE: The following is a fictional account based on factual data.

Published by Abdo & Daughters, 6535 Cecilia Circle, Edina, Minnesota 55439

Library bound edition distributed by Rockbottom Books, Pentagon Tower, P.O. Box 36036, Minneapolis, Minnesota 55435

Library of Congress Number: 90-082627   ISBN: 0-939179-85-7

Cover Photo by: Bettmann News Photos
Inside Photos by: The Bettmann News Photos

Edited by: John C. Hamilton

FORWARD — THE WARNING

SUNDAY, SEPTEMBER 17,1989
Christiansted, St. Croix, U.S. Virgin Islands

Just arrived on St. Croix. We (myself and two photographers) have been assigned to report on the hurricane headed this way — Hugo.

I've never seen a hurricane, but from the way people are reacting here, they're taking it very seriously. Business and home owners are taping up or nailing boards over their windows. Grocery store shelves are emptying fast — food in cans and boxes is going, and the bottled water is gone. Hardware stores were attacked by scores of people buying additional flashlights and batteries. We're set up in our hotel with these items, too. I've got a large supply of batteries that I'm carrying with my recorder. I'm going to report everything that's happening, as it's happening. Now, it's just a matter of waiting for the storm to come in.

Forecasters are warning that Hugo is "extremely dangerous." Although I've never actually experienced a hurricane, I've done my research:

Fact - Hurricanes are revolving tropical storms with winds of at least 74 miles per hour. Hugo is said to have winds of up to 140 mph.

Fact - "Hurricane" comes from the Yucatan's Carib Indians' god of violent storms and thunderbolts: "Huracan." The terms huracan, hurricane, cyclone, and typhoon all mean the same. The National Weather Service began giving the storms women's names in 1953. Only recently have men's names also been used — i.e., "Hugo."

Fact - Hurricanes occur most frequently in the summer and fall when ocean water temperatures peak. The storms draw their power from the water's heat. Once they hit land, the heat is gone, and they weaken and rain themselves out.

Fact - A hurricane can have a diameter of 700 miles (about the distance between New York and Chicago!). Hugo is spread over an arc 600 miles wide.

Fact - Hurricanes can cause waves in excess of 25 feet above normal. Hugo is sending waves shooting 10 feet high. These high waves attack the land along with heavy rains. A single area can have 20-30 inches of rain dropped on it. Flash flooding and mud slides are serious problems, and in fact, statistics show that 90% of the deaths associated with hurricanes are from drowning.

Just thinking about all this is making me nervous. The winds have come up here, although everything is still clear. Forecasters are predicting that if the storm stays on its course, it should hit here in about 8 hours — 6:00 p.m. tonight. It's a wait and see thing.

HURRICANE HUGO!

SUNDAY, SEPTEMBER 17, 1989
4:30 p.m.

St. Croix is such a beautiful place. The white beaches, clear blue ocean, warm sand and bright sun. The hotels and condos are clearly designed (and priced) for the rich. However, if you look beyond the wealth in the city and beaches, most of the islanders are very poor. They live in rundown homes and struggle to survive. There is a sharp contrast between them and the vacationers.

Still, the main source of income on the island is tourism, so naturally that's what makes jobs. Yet islanders must dislike the wealthy people who come in to stay for a week or two and live like kings, when they have to struggle just to make ends meet. So much for "paradise."

This island looks like it'll be going through some changes. Everyone we've talked to believes Hugo's going to hit hard. Reports are that the storm is moving in slowly — only travelling about 9-12 mph. However, it is heading directly for us.

The streets are emptying. Many stores have closed. (Emergency supplies are nearly sold out, anyway.) The shelves are bare. We've stocked in pretty well. I believe we'll go back to the hotel, have dinner, and wait for the storm.

7:00 p.m.
The winds are coming up. Palm trees are beginning to bend. People aren't exactly frightened yet, but they definitely look concerned. Lots of excitement and nervous laughter from the guests gathered in the lobby of our hotel. It's getting darker outside, too. Rains are beginning.

Several people left to take shelter in the high school. It's certainly the safer place to be, although if we want to report on the storm, we have to be where we can see what's happening. The hotel manager has reassured us that the hotel has stood through previous storms, and has been built to withstand heavy winds. We're counting on that construction to get us through this.

9:30 p.m.

It's hard to be heard over the wind . . . I'm shouting into my recorder . . . Anything loose in the street, garbage, papers, pieces of clothing, everything is flying by.

There go the lights! The electrical lines must have blown down. It's pitch black in here. Like being deep in a cave — only much more frightening with the wind screaming outside.

The hotel has emergency generators, powered by batteries, and we've retrieved our flashlights. Usually, at night, you have the soft light of the stars and the moon. Right now, the storm is blocking out everything around us. It's like a sinister dark monster roaring and thrashing out violently at everything in its reach. The only thing between us and this monster "Hugo" are the thin walls of our hotel!

10:00 p.m.

It's getting later and more frightening. It almost seems like an earthquake. Everything is shaking apart. The glass windows and doors, although taped and in some places boarded-up, are very vulnerable. Between the pounding rain and the shrieking wind, even small rocks are hurled against the walls with enough force to sound like bombs. This has become a war . . . a war between nature and man. All we can do is hope to survive.

11:00 p.m.
The rains are falling so hard you can no longer distinguish objects (posts, trees, anything) only inches from the door. It's like a wall of hard, pounding water, and it's trying to get at us.

There's been talk of evacuating to the high school, but we couldn't leave now. If one could even get the door open against the wind, you'd be swept away in seconds. I'm beginning to see how foolish it was to stay here. This story isn't worth my life!

MONDAY, SEPTEMBER 18, 1989
12:05 a.m.
This is one **bad** Monday! There'll be no sleeping tonight. It looks like the walls are "breathing."

They're moving in and out against the force of the wind and the air pressure inside and outside the hotel. I'm not sure if some of those glass doors are going to make it, either. They look like they're going to cave in.

People are terrified. I think we're all suddenly realizing that this is not a scary ride at the county fair, where you can get off after three minutes. This hurricane is for real. Our lives are truly in danger . . .

BANG! . . . Oh, no! Part of the hotel's roof just ripped away. The roaring noise is so loud. I hope I'll be able to transcribe this tape later. I hope I'll be alive to transcribe it!

1:30 a.m.
They brought down a couple people from upstairs. The wind took the roof off right over their heads. They're drenched. One man has several cuts from flying glass. I think they're in shock. I'm going over to help. The main thing is to keep them warm.

2:30 a.m.

Water is starting to rise. I keep remembering that 90% of people killed in hurricanes die from drowning. We're not far from shore. The hotel has a ham radio, and we've been listening to reports around the island. It doesn't sound good. We've got waves as high as 10 feet hitting the beach! Yachts have been washed inland. Cars and buses washed away.

3:00 a.m.

It's quieting. The storm is moving on. The rain is still falling, but the roar has stopped . . . outside, at least. I can still hear it. My ears are ringing and I can't make them stop. All-in-all, though, it looks like we've made it through OK. I'm exhausted. I have to lay down — even if it's just for an hour . . .

AFTER HUGO — DEVASTATION!

MONDAY, SEPTEMBER 18, 1989
5:30 a.m.

The sun is coming out. It's great to see light again, but I can hardly describe the devastation! The city of Christiansted looks like it is part of a war zone. It's hard to believe that this was the same beautiful city of yesterday. Rather, it looks like Hugo picked us up and deposited us in some wasteland.

There's broken glass and splintered wood everywhere. Overturned cars and uprooted trees. The beautiful white beach of yesterday is littered with garbage: sea plants and dead fish, trees, and miles of twisted wreckage from homes and businesses. Whole houses were swept away — only the floors remain.

7:00 a.m.

Radio operators have reported three people dead and 97% of the buildings on the island damaged. Winds hit at 160 mph. The island is only 84-

Personal belongings can be seen in the rooms of this condominium which had the roof blown off when Hurricane Hugo slammed into it.

square-miles big, but everywhere you look, there's destruction. The hotel lost the roof and a few windows. There'll be water damage and some rebuilding, but it held fast. Thank goodness. There were many times last night that I thought, "This is the end."

9:00 a.m.
It's beginning to get warm; muggy and uncomfortable. Lots of standing water and puddles — but no clean running water. Power lines are still down. I doubt if they'll have any electricity restored today. The same is true for the telephone lines. Most all boats have been beached, sunk, wrecked or swamped. The airport is in ruins — planes overturned or twisted in huge pieces of junk metal.

Except for the ham radio operators, we are cut off from the rest of the world. From what little information we can gather, Hugo is heading for Puerto Rico. Because of all the devastation, we won't be able to get off the island to track it, but I think there's more of a story right here. Recovery is going to be difficult. I hope help is on the way.

14

Traffic moves slow past a row of power lines blown over by Hurricane Hugo.

1:00 p.m.

Looters! As we're walking around the city, we're seeing a lot of theft going on. There are gangs of looters, some even carrying machetes and guns. Any store left unattended is a target. So many buildings have been damaged, it's easy for people to walk right in and take what they want. And that's just what they're doing.

In some cases, it looks like people are searching for essentials: food, bottled drinks, etc. However, we're at one of the shopping centers, and people are walking in with empty bags and coming out with everything from electronics to jewelry to clothing.

2:00 p.m.

We've heard that Hugo is hitting Puerto Rico. I hope they're prepared for the worst, because that's what's coming.

4:00 p.m.

I thought last night was frightening. I'm fearing for my life again today! The island is out of control.

16

People stand behind a keep out sign in front of yachts which washed ashore, afraid violent looting would break out.

A cleanup crew works at the airport as a DC-3 airplane rests on a hanger after being lifted there by the 120 mile per hour winds of Hurricane Hugo.

There aren't anywhere near enough police or National Guardsmen to take charge. People are carrying shotguns and .38 pistols in the streets! Some store owners have put up signs warning that they'll "shoot to kill" anyone who approaches their property. This seems the only way to stop the looting. I know that in some ways, the people feel this is their chance to get some things they never could have. They figure the store's insurance will cover the losses. One thing's for sure, I'm not going to approach any of these people and try to explain that stealing is still stealing!

We've decided to stay off the streets for the rest of the night. I'm afraid of being attacked. There have been several groups of islanders yelling and threatening us. When is help going to arrive?!

8:00 p.m.
It's quiet. Last night was so loud you wanted to cover your ears. Now it's so quiet, you strain to hear something . . . anything . . . BANG! BANG! BANG! . . . except that! We've heard some gunfire like this every hour or so. I don't even

want to think about what's going on. There are so many homeless people out there. Frightened, hungry, unprotected. I want to do something, but I don't know what. Something has to be done. The Virgin Islands are part of the United States. I don't understand why we haven't received any assistance yet. This is terrifying.

TUESDAY, SEPTEMBER 19,1989
9:00 a.m.

Our supplies are beginning to run low. We're rationing what's left of the water — that's what I'm most concerned about. As far as I've seen, there's been no aid sent to the island. I don't know what's taking so long.

We are out this morning, although we're being very careful about where we go. The shopping center is in ruins. I've seen a few shops still intact in other places, but the owners are staying there. One man allowed us to approach. He had a sign out front that read: "Keep out or you will be shot." He had been protecting his store all night long, and he said that he fired a few warning shots at intruders.

1:00 p.m.

I've heard that some 600 people got off the island — all fearing for their lives. I've talked with other reporters just arriving by helicopter. They said that vacationers from the mainland U.S. met them as they landed and begged to be airlifted out.

As for Hugo . . . From ham radio reports, much of Puerto Rico is a disaster area. We've heard of 14 deaths and nearly 30,000 people made homeless. And it's not over yet! Apparently Hugo's zig-zagging out over the Atlantic Ocean. That means that it's building power from the warm waters there. Its course shows it headed toward the United States — possibly Florida or the Carolina's.

3:00 p.m.

One free-lance photographer actually swam out to a Coast Guard boat patrolling just off the island. He wanted to get off the island even worse than I do. What I really want to do now is to finish my story and go home. But I've made it this long, I'm staying until things get better.

6:00 p.m.

Rumor has it that a group of prison inmates from a nearby jail escaped and are terrorizing the streets. Nothing is safe from looters. I've even seen some National Guardsmen packing goods into their trucks and taking off. I suppose they could be holding it for the owners . . . but, somehow, I doubt it.

8:00 p.m.

In talking to some residents here, they believe that the looting has happened because there has been no aid; no help from the outside world. It's true that many of these people have lost everything. They need food and clothing and materials to rebuild their homes . . .

WEDNESDAY, SEPTEMBER 20, 1989
9:00 a.m.

Another morning and no new changes — still no power, telephone service, or clean water. The situation is strictly survival for the 53,000 people living here. What are the homeless to do? And the injured? How can the hospitals help? And with the looting and threats, people are in danger just being on the streets.

We're still trying to help — giving assistance where we can, listening, cleaning up, yet staying out of the way when any large groups of people come near.

2:00 p.m.
Help — finally! Over 1,000 U.S. military police arrived. They immediately took to the streets, as did we, following them. From what I could tell, the Virgin Island's governor, Alexander Farrelly, claimed that he didn't request any help. Not request help!? Help is needed desperately here! They have to regain control.

3:30 p.m.
Coast Guard crewmen also came ashore. It's beginning to feel safer . . . Many people are still begging to get off the island. This is still a disaster area. Communication lines are opening up. All that's left is to rebuild the damage — that could take months and millions of dollars.

We've heard that Hugo is headed for South Carolina, and so are we. We're taking a press helicopter back to the mainland. In some ways, I can't believe I'm doing this. I thought we were going to die last Sunday. Now, I'm putting myself in that same danger. Still — I want to see what happens . . .

HUGO HITS THE MAINLAND

THURSDAY, SEPTEMBER 21, 1989
Charleston, South Carolina
6:00 p.m.
We're in Charleston, South Carolina, and Hugo's not far behind. There are a lot of reporters, photographers and TV crews here. It seems like a media convention, although I think everyone is aware of the danger — residents and journalists alike.

Another beautiful city preparing for the worst. Charleston is 311 years old. Unfortunately, I've seen what can happen when Hugo visits your town. The next day — the beauty is gone.

Now the town is boarded up. People have either left the city and gone inland (something people on a small island obviously can't do), or have decided to ride out the storm in their homes or central shelters in schools, hospitals, and federal buildings. We are in the City Hall, and the winds are really building.

8:00 p.m.
Hurricane-force winds outside. Everything is a blur of rushing winds. Power lines are down, trees are snapping, and the waves are so high, they're flooding the streets and roadways. Hugo has definitely arrived!

12:00 p.m.
I was just feeling safe inside this 188-year-old brick building — no movement of the walls, like in the St. Croix hotel, when - BLAST! I think Hugo just cracked open the roof! Mayor Riley had been using this as the command post; now all our power is gone. We're OK, but water is pouring in . . .

FRIDAY, SEPTEMBER 22, 1989
7:00 a.m.

It was a fight for our lives. I dropped my recorder during the rush to help with the water. I'm borrowing another now. Hugo blasted Charleston last night and moved northward up the coast. Now it's a tropical storm, slowly raining itself out, ready to die.

The damage is horrifying. People are beginning to return, but they're returning to nothing but shattered skeletons of buildings that yesterday were their homes. Already, Charleston is a disaster area.

It's the worst hurricane to hit the United States since Hurricane Camille slammed into the Mississippi coast in 1969, killing 256 and doing $1.4 billion in damages. We don't have a death toll for sure yet, although I've heard 40. Certainly the warnings helped keep those numbers down, but it's still sad.

As for the damage, it'll cost billions of dollars to rebuild everything. The streets are flooded. Places that didn't get damaged from the 135 mile-an-hour winds got hit with flooding from the 17-foot waves of water. And if a building escaped that, there were also fires breaking out where broken natural gas pipes leaked and ignited.

People are canoeing on city streets. Bridges are twisted and useless. Some roads are completely gone — either washed away or covered in thick mud. There are cars and washers and dryers and refrigerators all floating down roadways. Windows are shattered. Roofs are splintered and gone. Chimneys have shattered brick-by-brick.

Power and utilities are out in 85% of the city. However, unlike St. Croix, emergency help has been quick in coming. Already there are Red Cross and emergency aid stations set up. The city has been declared a disaster area and federal funds are being issued. Some looting has taken place, but very little. National Guard troops were called in immediately to patrol the area.

While the devastation is about the same as on St. Croix, being part of the United States will make the cleanup quicker and more efficient. The worst part is dealing with the recovery. All the money in the world won't bring back the dead (40 looks to be the latest figure), nor will money return the historic buildings that have withstood hundreds of years of Mother Nature's worst fury . . . until now.

Light aircraft litter the end of the run way at the airport.

It's hard to describe the fear and hopelessness of the last week. I can leave it all behind — go home. But the people of the Virgin Islands, Puerto Rico, and South Carolina won't forget Hugo. Not for many, many years to come.

I have learned a lot about how people take care of each other; and how they turn on each other. I've gained a new respect for nature's fury. And I've come to know fear: the powerful horror of a hurricane.

Hurricane Hugo's powerful winds left the cities it hit devastated.